THE ROOTS OF UNBELIEF

In Defense of Everything

THE ROOTS OF UNBELIEF
In Defense of Everything

by
William J. O'Malley, S.J.

150
OM

PAULIST PRESS/DEUS BOOK
New York, N.Y./Paramus, N.J.

NIHIL OBSTAT:
Rev. Joseph M. Jankowiak, S.T.D.
Censor Deputatus

IMPRIMATUR:
Most Rev. Joseph L. Hogan, D.D., S.T.D.
Bishop of Rochester
October 16, 1975

Library of Congress
Catalog Card Number: 75-34840

ISBN: 0-8091-1915-3

Published by Paulist Press
Editorial Office: 1865 Broadway, N.Y., N.Y. 10023
Business Office: 400 Sette Drive, Paramus, N.J. 07652

Printed and bound in the
United States of America.

CONTENTS

For Bob Edelman
who keeps me on my toes
which is the best place from which
to dance.

1. THE TAPROOT: CALCULATED IGNORANCE

After the gift of existence, what's the first gift a baby gets? A good hard slap on the butt!

It makes him cry, but it also makes him breathe for the first time. The seeming cruelty of the doctor makes the baby *want* air. The baby doesn't *know* it's air he needs. He doesn't ponder the options and decide to breathe. Its breath he needs, and whether or not he wants to belong to a world where air is necessary and lungs have to pump, he's jolted into reaching for it.

Human beings can stay in the womb only so long or they atrophy. So, by the nature of birth the mother's body rejects the fetus-come-to-term, and forces it from the warm and passive comfort of the womb into a cold world where it is greeted with a slap and with its first attempt to face need by itself and with its first personal struggle to satisfy that need.

That little biological overture really contains all the themes I hope to touch on in these pages: just as the body by its very nature needs air and the effort of breathing, the spirit by its very nature needs God

1

and the effort of prayer. If one starves the body, the body dies; if one starves the spirit, the spirit dies.

Before going further, it might be good if I clarify what I mean by "spirit." Everyone knows what a human body is: the vehicle that carries us around, the means by which we take in data and by which we express what we think and who we are; it is fed by the bodies of other animals, by the vegetation of the earth, by air and sunshine and the physical stimuli of light, color, sound, texture, odor and temperature.

Everyone knows what the human mind is: the central station in which we turn the physical stimuli into ideas, forge judgments, hammer out conclusions, store information, dream dreams, organize our lives, plan, fabricate; it is fed by the minds of other men and women, by the concretized experience of the ideas of history and of the world we inhabit, by the evidence of our own bodily senses.

But not too many people know what the human spirit is. It is that elusive element in a human being that cannot be confined to the body or to the brain— or even to a combination of the two. It is the aspect of humanity that makes us more than computers that can move around by themselves, the "place" within us where we encounter the mysterious, the not-fully-explainable, the holy. Here is where we love—a reality that far surpasses the capacities of mere bodies and brains; here is the source of joy, self-sacrifice, cruelty, honor, ambition, hope, trust. The human mind and body can fabricate machines and pots and clothing; they are practical, this-world. But it is the human spirit that creates whole *new* worlds like Elsinore and Never-Never Land and 1984.

In a word, the human spirit is the "I" that stands behind all that the body and the mind do. The human spirit is my soul, my *self*.

The human body, like the animal's, is made to cope with space. The human mind, unlike the animal's, is made to cope with time. But the human spirit, although it is anchored for the moment in space and time, is free to soar—if it dares—into eternal moments that are free of time and space. In those ecstatic moments when we are filled with joy beyond the power of words to capture it, moments when we know beyond question we are loved, that we have succeeded against all odds, there is a fullness in us that no longer has any relation to time or space, to body or mind. We don't need watches and maps in those moments; we are "there," beyond bodies and minds.

The hungers of the human body make themselves known from the moment of birth, and as long as there is food around, the normal human body needs no prodding to keep feeding itself. If it eats inferior food it will be a sickly body—spindly or flabby —but it will stay alive. Sort of. The hungers of the human mind make themselves known almost as soon, and the baby looks around with thirsty eyes drinking in everything, and within its first two years it has accumulated an enormous amount of information with a speed no computer could sustain. After that, our infinitely variegated world keeps offering food to the mind. If the mind also eats inferior food, it will be a sickly mind—spindly or flabby—but it will stay alive. Sort of.

The hungers of the spirit grow more slowly. From the moment of birth, the baby's body craves mere body contact. As it grows, it is enough that it knows other bodies are around. But it is not until adolescence that the youngster begins to feel a loneliness that can corrode him inside even when he is in a crush of bodies. It is the time he begins to understand vaguely that people are not merely bodies, not even merely mental presences; they are persons. And that is a mystery. He tries to get at that mystery through his body, and he fails. He tries to isolate that mysterious person through his mind, and he fails. And if that third power, the power of the spirit, has had no food, no solitude, no wonder with which to nourish it, he will very likely stay on that frustrated body-mind level—or only a little above it—until he dies. The sexual pleasures of the body and the analytic pleasures of the mind are all he has with which to contact the people and the world. And yet somewhere inside him he knows there is more, that neither body nor mind can penetrate into that mysterious inner core of the other.

It is for this reason, I think, that so many young people, no matter how liberated, have spiritless, joyless faces. It is for this reason, I think, that they drift away from organized religion, because it, too, seems able to use only the body and the mind to get at the mystery of what it is to be human and fulfilled. It is for this reason, too, I think, that so many young people in recent years have joined Eastern sects and communes, why they have plunged into hallucinogenics and other drugs—not to pander to their bodies, as so many dispirited adults would like to claim—but precisely to find the path to the powers in themselves that will transcend space and time.

The denial of the spirit, too, I think, is responsible for the fact that we treat the problems of the planet we inhabit as economic problems rather than as human problems. We speak of Saharan famine and ecological suicide and over-population in economic terms: jobs, balances of trade, meteorological statistics. And while Indian administrators store grain in large cities to be sold to the rich at high prices, while our rivers continue to stagnate in order to keep up employment, and fetuses are scraped out of wombs, human beings are dying. And they die in slow reversal: first the spirit fades away, then the mind gives up, then the body ceases to run anymore.

All of this is done, so we are told, in order to "keep up the standard of living." But that, of course, depends on what "living" means. If it means having a stereo, a car and a refrigerator full of frozen food, getting an education through college, then a great many Americans at least are doing very well indeed. But is that all that it means? Is there no difference between "living" and "being alive?"

In a world where the spirit is starved into uselessness, it is every man for himself. "If I can't get a profit on my cattle, I'll shoot them before I send them to the starving. *I* work for a living!" And not only a number of people die in India or Africa, but something in the herder who has shot his cattle dies a little too. If a man's spirit, his soul, his self is starved, it becomes very thin indeed. And if he is self-*centered*, he is feeding his spirit only with himself, devouring such thin fare that there is very little —if any—self left.

Why? Why would human beings starve their very *selves* to death? Surely they would not willingly starve their bodies. Surely they would not willingly starve their minds, even though they fed their minds little more than the popcorn of gossip columns and the chewing gum of television. But they seem most willing to starve their spirits, their souls, their selves. Why?

That's really what this book is all about.

It is my contention that spiritually most adolescents, and perhaps most adults, are still inside the womb, refusing to budge out into the bigger world that may be as transcendent and liberating as a book like the Gospels says, but it could also be one great big hoax. And the one great difference between the birth of the body and mind and the birth of the spirit is that this time one has a choice. The fetus nuzzling in the womb and the baby gobbling up sights and sounds didn't know what they were getting into, and they didn't have that much choice in the matter anyway—right? They were forced out, slapped, stuffed with food. Then, in the same way that Mommy had said, "Eat your carrots," Mommy and teacher were saying, "Eat your ABC's; eat your numbers." (They also had him baptized and took him to have his spirit fed in Church, but it wasn't something he could feel with his body, like carrots, or feel with his mind, like the alphabet.)

Then, in adolescence, comes the time he ratifies or rejects the feeding practices his parents chose in childhood when he was unable to choose for himself. At that time, almost all ratify the choice of food for the body, though perhaps not the same kinds of food that Mommy was always pushing. Far fewer ratify the choice of continuing to feed the mind on more and more difficult food. And sadly, nearly all refuse to ratify much further ingestion of food for the spirit.

But the spirit—even if its existence is denied, even if it is walled off behind noise and passivity and pretense from the solitude and challenge that could make it grow—remains hungry.

By the nature of the human being, by the way we are made, if one barricades the human spirit inside a self-protective womb, the body can live and thrive, the mind can live and thrive, but one begins to die as a human. So God, like the wise physician, the wise father, the wise teacher, will very often jerk us up short with pain and suffering and loss, eject us from the womb, slap us into breathing the real air for ourselves. He jolts us into reaching for a larger life than we may have planned to live.

The deepest reason for unbelief is simple: We love comfort and fear risk. We are hooked into the comfy womb: the body—and, for some, the mind—is enough. And as mankind progresses materially and invents all sorts of new protections and dodges and escapes to fill the time, we become more and more embedded in that womb, more safely withdrawn into our tiny world, more shrewdly adept at avoiding suffering. We become so canny that we can avoid even the suffering that will make us grow, like the toil of reaching out to the poor, the lame, the halt and the blind; like the toil of reading and thinking for oneself; like the toil of wrestling for one's dignity as a person without unremitting escapes into booze or pot or masturbation or TV or casual sex; like the toil of attempting personal communication with an invisible God who is so often so silent.

I find wise sayings in the least likely places, and I found one in the light comedy, *The Teahouse of the August Moon*. Sakini, the little Okinawan interpreter says, "Pain make man think. Thought make man wise. Wisdom make life endurable." But when we are so cautiously shielded from pain, either our own or others', there is no chance for wisdom. When we are shielded from thought, by witless media presentations, by teachers too timid to challenge and by our own inertia, there is no chance for wisdom. And without wisdom, life becomes unendurable unless, of course, life itself—real life—can be avoided by filling one's days with trivialities and making them seem important: styles, ballscores, movie gossip, cars, competition, Monday night football, money. It's all very plastic, but if we all get together and agree to put our minds in neutral and kid one another, we can pretend it's gold, just as we can pretend that green paper, properly printed, is a true indication of value. It's what T.S. Eliot called "living—or partly living." It's an imitation of aliveness, but if no one else has anything better than we have, why should we worry? Besides, it's tangible; it's womb-like; it's secure. We become too busy living—or partly living—to find out what living is for.

The taproot of unbelief in both teenagers and adults is, very simply, calculated ignorance—a self-blinding that is the ultimate protection against the loss of the comfortable womb. "What I don't know can't hurt me." (Which is one reason, I suspect, why so many people buy a Bible and never open it.) And the sturdy growth of this ignorance is ably aided and abetted by the fundamental law of human nature: inertia. "Any body (or mind, or spirit) at rest will stay at rest until it is affected by some force outside itself."

To overcome ignorance and its doting guardian, inertia, takes thinking, reading, probing, brooding, deciding, risking—in a word: effort. Not just the minimal effort of putting food prepared by someone else into one's body, nor putting facts predigested by someone else's mind into one's own mind, but searching. Wrestling. Doubting. And thus the words of the cliché remain now and forever true, "Many men would rather die than think. Most of them do."

This then is the taproot of unbelief in God or at least of the so-called "vacationing Catholic"; it is the calculated ignorance of the truth. But even further, growing out of this taproot of calculated ignorance that is fed by rich deposits of natural inertia, I think I can discern at least five hardy young shoots branching upwards and outwards towards a flourishing disbelief: (1) Ignorance of being gifted with life, and therefore of the need to be grateful; (2) Ignorance of sin, and therefore of the need for salvation (whatever that means); (3) Ignorant contentment with a false god, materialism, that offers a cosy comfort far more desirable than the fiery challenge and joy of the fierce Galilean; (4) Ignorance of death, and therefore of the need for a dimension to our lives larger than the tangible; and (5) Ignorant fear of large communities, and therefore a settling for a small, dull but safe life.

How much easier it must have been for stupider men and women, before the world was asphalted over and clogged with smoke, when they lived on the land—families with the old people sharing hard-won wisdom with the young, and the young giving hope and long, rich life to the old. It is the secret voice within us that responds to *The Waltons* on TV each week, a voice fought down by the new-found sophistication that calls it all saccharine and naive—yet we yearn for it.

It was far less comfortable then. Less clean, but less cluttered. Less exciting, but less dull. There men and women wrestled with the uncompromising earth and elements, but the grain rising golden from the earth was—as it was to Jesus—the miracle of rebirth, the reward for struggle. Such men and women knew mystery. They knew awe. They knew God.

Today we wrestle not with the unpredictable land but with predictable machines and balance sheets and course outlines. There is no chancy struggle for rebirth, only tomorrow. Maybe. There is no mystery, only problems. There is no awe, only novelty. There is no God, only us. Clinging together. Alone.

In the Depression it was easier for men and women to believe and thereby to grow as selves because they knew they were weak, knew death and their need to be saved, knew life in themselves and in their children and in their crops to be a precarious gift, knew the joy and fulfillment of risk, knew only one God who could not be sold for money. They knew that they, even collectively, did not have all the answers.

In growing more sophisticated, I wonder if we haven't bargained away salvation and awe and gratitude and joy and risk for comfort. In keeping up with the Joneses, have we perhaps become so like *them* that we failed to keep up with ourselves? All around me I see kids and adults wrestling with who they are as unique persons while, at the same time, focusing the majority of their effort on being like everybody else. But belief means taking a stand no matter what anyone else thinks. Belief means making a bet; a bet one can lose. It means living with the excitement of uncertainty and unpredictability. Belief means having no permanent roots at all, except in the One who calls.

Is it any wonder that the number of believers is diminishing?

I have said that I think the taproot of this self-impoverishing disbelief is a *calculated* ignorance. I think we willingly blind ourselves to our basic needs (or try to) simply to shield ourselves from the consequence: uncertainty. Rather than ask *why* we feel so useless, unloved, unlovable, we plaster creams and goos and sprays and nards over every bodily crevice and cranny, hoping to cover our supposed ugliness with masks. Rather than make the painful effort to discover *why* we're acting like bastards all the time, we temporarily anesthetize ourselves with a bottle of pills or booze. Rather than analyze *why* life seems such a crashing bore, such a deadening rat race, we turn on the TV and bore ourselves to sleep. Rather than acknowledge that the body and mind are not enough, that there is still an emptiness within us, we try to fill the emptiness with airy promises and unrealizable dreams and wishful thinking.

A person doesn't seek food until he admits to hunger. He doesn't venture out in search of something unless he acknowledges his own need. He doesn't try to communicate in his spirit to a God beyond time and space when he "has everything he could want right here, thank you."

Like the baby in the womb, we feel we have everything we want and need right here, even when we really don't, even when we know in our heart of hearts that we can't stay "here" forever. But the general comfort can smother the itch for more. It is only at the moment when he feels hunger that the Prodigal heads for home.

In the hope that one or two spirits will risk coming out and living, let me take the roots of unbelief one at a time and, again, hopefully, slap a few bottoms into a few angry cries, but cries that suck in the searing Spirit of God.

2. IGNORANCE OF BEING GIFTED

If we are truly the children of God, we are very spoiled children indeed. Not only does he dotingly drown us with gifts but, brats that we are, we grow to take them for granted, almost as if they were our due, almost as if we had done something to *deserve* them.

As we grow older, more sophisticated, more distant from childish wonder, we don't stand in awe of popes or presidents or parents any longer. Whereas a child looks round-eyed at the clowns and at Santa Claus and even at an ordinary old horse in the street, we sniff with patient boredom even at landings on the moon and the death of entire nations from famine. We have grown to know better; the world has lost its ability to surprise.

Milt Kamen, the comedian, said something very wise to me one time, "We've lost the taste of bread." And he's right. Food has no flavor for us anymore unless it burns; drink has no taste unless it has a kicker. It's no wonder that bread and wine seem so insipid as symbols of life.

Who cares about fresh air, until it's threatened with pollutants? Who can eat plain bread—without

14

butter or jelly or peanut butter or raisins or meat or mayonaisse—unless there is nothing else, unless he is ravenous? Who looks at his life, or the lives of those he loves, as gifts he did nothing to deserve, gifts he should rejoice over, unless life is threatened by a sickness or death he can't control? How many of us wait too long to say, "I love you?"

Most of us are reasonably healthy, reasonably well-fed, reasonably well-clothed. And, if we thank anybody, whom do we thank?—the doctor who brings us back to health, the statesmen who keep peace? Who writes a letter to thank Henry Kissinger? Hell, that's what they get paid for, and damn well-paid, too! Do we thank the farmer, the miller, the railroad worker, the pizza maker, the salesgirl? Hell, that's what *they* get paid for. Do we thank the boss who gives us the money to pay for all these things? Hell, he gets his pound of flesh out of me every week. I pay 'em all! I've got a right!

But whom do we pay for the air and the sun and the stars? Whom do we pay for the people we love so much, who need never have been born? Whom do we pay for the gift of waking up in the morning because surely people worthier than you or I did not wake up? Chesterton said that children are grateful to Santa Claus for the oranges they find in their stockings on Christmas morning. But whom do we thank for the legs we found in our stockings *this* morning?

Really, we began growing selfish right from the beginning, didn't we? Who ever thinks of thanking his mother for carrying him nine months in her belly with all the discomfort and inconvenience and pain that meant? Who ever sends a gift to his mother on *his* birthday—in gratitude for the gift of all gifts, the gift without which there could have been no other gifts—life? Who ever thanks his father for all he went without—not just material things, but his freedom? Who ever thanked the grammar-school teacher who taught him to read?

Well, in a sense, no thanks were needed or expected. A mother, a father, a teacher gives and nourishes life because it's in their nature, because they love easily. No good mother sitting up with a sick child thinks even for an instant of what a sacrifice it is, "what this kid owes me." In fact, that's how you can tell the good parents and teachers from the bad ones: the kids owe me nothing for my sake. "I loved doing it; it has been my life. To tell you the truth, I'm grateful to them for letting me give, for drawing me out, for accepting my gift of myself."

But—and it's a big but—the kids *do* owe something to those who give them life and amplify it, perhaps not for the parents' sake or the teachers' sakes but for the *kid's* sake. Surely I am less a man, less human and meaner-spirited if I accept a gift of love and feel no need even to say thanks even once. And I don't mean the obligatory times when custom and the greed of merchandisers require that a gift be given, as for Christmas, birthdays, Father's day. I mean the inner conviction that one has been gifted, and the joy of the gift fills me to bursting with gratitude.

Of course, if one feels he *deserved* to be given life, it is not a gift at all, it is payment for services rendered. ("You got *me* out of it, didn't you, you lucky dogs?") And there is little joy in having such a "gift."

Again, then, whom does one thank for existence itself? How easily we forget that we were not around to pay the price for existence. True, had I never existed, I would never have known my loss. But I *do* exist, and because I might have missed all this, I must thank someone! Not for his sake. He doesn't need thanks, and like my parents' share in the gift of my existence the part God played was the fruit of love. But I need to be grateful for *my* sake.

So often I have offered the gift of love to people who made me realize that I was not loved in return, or at least not as much as I was offering. For all my tricks, I couldn't force them to love me. I couldn't *make* it happen. As a result, when someone obviously does return my love, undeniably does love me in return, I realize I am receiving something I could never command. So I'm grateful, and my gratitude makes my joy all the greater; I have to find expression for both my joy and my gratitude. When I'm loved, I want to say thanks for that gift, not just once but again and again.

In the same way I cannot command the giving or taking away of my life. But it was obviously given and it will obviously be taken away. So I'm grateful, even if the gift is precarious—or especially because it is precarious—and my gratitude makes my joy the greater; I have to say thanks for my existence, not just once, but again and again.

However, like spoiled children, we take the

Giver of the gift of life for granted. We go our merry
way without a single serious thought of him. Only
when we are in need do we go to him, all tears and
pleas and protestations of love, our bribes and bar-
gains all neatly prepared. And, oddly, he is never insulted—as we in our pettiness would be—by the fact
that when times are good, he is forgotten; then, when
times are bad, we are back to panhandle again. He
becomes the lightswitch God who exists only when I
need him—and surely I don't need him for existence
any more. He's already given me that. The real question is what has he done for me lately?

At moments when existence is threatened, or
when our attention is called to the fragility of that
gift, we admit our need to be grateful. But at other
times—most times—we wrap ourselves in that calculated ignorance and choose to forget. It's unpleasant
to keep remembering that we are indebted, that we
are not independent and sufficient unto ourselves. It
makes us nervous to be beholden to Someone.

This, I suspect, is one of the subconscious reasons why many people find weekly Mass a drag. It's
not just that the service is so often boring—which,
too often, it is. There's a further feeling that, "Okay!
I'm grateful! But why do I have to keep checking
back every week—like dropping in on my parole
board or visiting a rich maiden aunt so she'll remember me in her will?" Such an attitude is not
necessarily a posture of ingratitude if gratitude
means, "All right. You gave me a present and I gave
you a present and now we're square, right?" Once

again, that is not gratitude as I see it; it's a business proposition, a *quid pro quo.* And in this particular case, we are talking about the gift of existence—the gift without which there could have been no further gifts. In that sense at least, the Giver of existence gave us *everything.* How do you give an adequate return for everything?

But if a man or woman does not see that the foundation of human life is the relation of a dependent creature to his freely creating Creator, he or she will never find God. How could they? As long as one thinks existence "just happened"—like an accident, then there is no need to express any gratitude for anything. One's existence was just a lucky break.

If there is a radical cause for disbelief in young and old today, it is this: we cease to look on life as a gift. We are the spoiled brats of the universe who have our inheritance and can feel free to leave our Father's house to make it on our own.

Till our luck runs out.

3. IGNORANCE OF NEEDING SALVATION

Whenever you hear some clergyman preaching salvation, don't you sometimes say to yourself, "Wait a minute. Salvation from *what*? What dangers or evil am I heading for—or already in—that this self-righteous do-gooder is going to 'save' me from? Most of the things men and women needed salvation from before, we've either already been saved from our we have new, this-world saviors working on them."

Well, there are two kinds of evil—evil that originates outside the self and evil that originates inside a person.

Evils from Outside

Few will deny the need for saviors from the evils outside a person. Salvation from atomic annihilation? Well, yes, but man's collective common sense will save us from that. It's in the hands of statesmen and scientists, and I can forget that one. I have the need to be saved, but somebody's already got the job.

Salvation from cancer? World hunger? Ecological suicide? Hurricanes? Alcoholism? Loneliness? Acne? Well, scientists will take care of those too, along with the government. Look what they've done with polio shots and birth-control devices and TV for shut-ins. Look what they've done with cholera vaccines and "The Green Revolution"—except maybe in Africa and Asia and South America, which may be more than half the surface of the earth, but *I'm* not there. And I have the police to save me from robbery, and firemen to save me from arson, and insurance men to save me in case the police and firemen fail. In a sense, I can forget those evils too; I have saviors there too.

One has to admit a certain amount of truth in those defenses against the need for a savior from evils outside oneself. If God gave us intelligence, he surely expected us to use it to fend off annihilation and suffering. And the intelligence of men organized into scientific and political work forces around the world seems to have a better chance of conquering the world's problems than something as flimsy as prayer has! You will note, however, that in such statements the "redeemer problem" is all taken care of by somebody else, that the person speaking—who is not really unusual—is leaving it all to "them."

That too is not as selfish as it seems. Perhaps "realistic" would be a truer word than "selfish." Unless one has the enormous talents to get on top of even some of the world's problems, he can't hope to solve even one of them—famine or ignorance or pollution or indignity. And fretting with guilt over one's own impotence before these vast problems is an exercise in futility.

But such retirement from responsibility is selfish insofar as it implies that *everything* outside the walls of one's house can be taken care of by people one pays or people who are crazy enough to care about those things. We are, each of us, equal residents on this earth and, although one can't crusade for everything, one surely is obliged to crusade for something—if not for disarmament or a better sharing of the world's goods or penal reform, then at least for something manageable like *this* soup kitchen or that school or some other disadvantaged, forgotten group. Even if one is not moved by the motive of our common responsibility for the world, one ought to be moved at least by selfish motives because the one who crusades for nothing, stands up for nothing is diminished as a human person, and is in danger of becoming something as flabby and colorless as things that live in the safe darkness under rocks.

But crusading takes me out of my small world where I look large. Against the bigger background I begin to look smaller, and as soon as I look smaller, I am in danger of *feeling* smaller, feeling need, needing prayer. I am in danger of God.

It is no accident that such men as Dag Hammarskjold and Gerald Ford have been unashamed to say that they pray. They may be very "big" men, but before the enormity of the world they became responsible for, they knew that they were very small indeed. They felt the need for help, and so they sought it—not ready-made solutions nor a miracle from the sky—but the conviction that they are not alone. Self-delusive? Only a man or woman with enormous self-confidence and very small problems could say that.

Evils from Inside

But there are also moments when one at least feels that there is a source of evil inside himself. Salvation from sin? Well, that's more than likely what those self-righteous preachers are trying to sell, isn't it? And it's really the only evil one can't hand over to anyone else, right? And do you want to know how we're "saved" from that? Simple! We merely have to recognize that sin doesn't *exist*—no more than the Tooth Fairy or the Bogey Man or warts on your hands when you masturbate. All one has to do is convince himself that there is really no such thing as evil emanating from within and one needn't have to worry about it anymore, right? Who needs salvation from something that doesn't exist?

Note that I will not be talking about an abnormal guilt, scrupulosity, the torment of being defiled by actions that are no more than trivial faults scarcely worthy of attention. This is a sickness, an inability to see the world as it really is and, like any other faulty vision problem, it can be given to a physician. The normal man or woman takes such shortcomings in stride, noting them, trying to eradicate them, but not suffering paroxysms of guilt if they take some time to uproot.

What I am talking about could be described as "rubbery conscience," gradually *extending* the carefree response that a man or woman should have to trivial bad habits like biting one's nails, or losing one's temper under stress, and taking the same breezy attitude to more serious faults like sleeping around, casually thoughtless destruction of other people's reputations, dishonesty. "Everybody does it. Why get uptight? Those are 'sins' invented by a Puritan church that thought being sinless was more important than being alive. Such things are only human."

Some of the so-called logical defenses of the "rubbery conscience" are the following.

Morality Changes

"They" say that there's really no such thing as sin anymore. Such ideas were okay for savages scared half out of their wits by taboos and medicine men, or for Victorian hypocrites who saw sins everywhere, even in bad table manners, just to make themselves look terrific. That was okay for scaring little kids in grammar school with devils and hell and punishment to keep them in line. But let's get serious, huh? We're grown up. This is almost 2000 A.D. We've come a long way from the totem pole!

There is something to be said for the position that things have changed. Many actions thought sinful years ago were influenced by uncritical taboos. But as I write, I find it hard to think of a specific, real "sin"—something more than provocative ankles —that wise men ever used to consider deadly and now consider trivial. Oh, perhaps usury, but most of the people I deal with don't even know what the word "usury" means. What I think these people are talking about are actions they would *like* to prove were forbidden only by primitive, unsophisticated taboos: extra-marital sex was taboo because they didn't have the pill, and therefore you might have a baby; cheating and shoplifting were taboo because they didn't have big corporations then which could easily absorb the loss.

But as soon as they say "because," they are saying that this is *the* reason why such-and-such action was taboo: namely, that in those far-off ignorant days, free sex or free pilferage of ideas or goods hurt another person but now don't hurt anyone. Those arguments don't convince me in the least, probably because far more often than these novice moralists, I've tried helplessly to console someone who *has* been recently hurt by extra-marital sex (not by pregnancy but by giving themselves totally to someone who lost interest and had made no real commitment). I also have tried, very often helplessly, to console someone who *has* been recently hurt by casual cheating (not by being the guilty party but the innocent one, who was the only one caught).

People who argue this way, it seems to me, always have a personal axe to grind. Either they have some pet "sin" they don't want to give up, or

they feel oppressed by any authority that is going to
point out their sins and faults and shortcomings, and
therefore they crave freedom from all parents, teachers, bosses and spouses. If they can deny that any
evil exists, if they can lay the blame for their guilt
feelings onto some outmoded taboo, then they can
go on their merry way with their little pet (so-called)
sins, and they can say to hell with authority and all
its dirty commandments and laws and guilt com-
plexes that stifle human life instead of liberating it.

I suspected that this was why one day in class
one of the very brightest boys I've ever taught said
one of the very stupidest things I've ever heard: "The
nature of man has changed so much in just the last
hundred years that none of the rules that applied
then apply now."

Surely there must have been some kind of ulterior motive to make such a smart kid so easily put
out his own eyes, as it were.

For one thing, the nature of man has not
changed so much that he is now free of the "law" of
gravity or the "laws" of genetics or the "law" of the
jungle. Surely there are *some* moral imperatives that
have not changed, some laws within each of us from
which even technological progress has not liberated
us. I doubt, for instance, that we would be any more
tolerant of child-battering than a Victorian or
Roman or a bushman would have been, especially if
the child were one's own. We are no more willing
today to wipe out any strictures against incest than
Oedipus was. We are even less and less able to live
with an acceptance of war and genocide as a means

to settle our differences—less able than Alexander or David or Caesar or Attila or Charlemagne or Stalin. On the contrary, although the realizations come with intolerable slowness, the more history progresses, the more *in*tolerant we become of such actions.

Except when they affect us.

When I engage in premarital sex—or when my friends do—it's understandable: we're young; we're in love; we're repressed all day and need some release; it's natural; why should all the Playboys and Playgirls have all the fun while we keep our pants zipped and live like nice little boys and girls, like little priests and nuns? This works until the first guy comes up and tells me what his friend "got off" of my sister; until the first guy "takes advantage" of my daughter. When he does it against someone I love, it's a sin; when I do it, well. . . . Strange, since every girl is somebody's daughter.

The same is true of cheating. When I cheat it's understandable: oh, God, it's only human isn't it? Everybody does it. Until someone cheats me. Even then it's odd how the calculated ignorance fails to see that fairness is a *two*-way street, that if I demand that even big companies and the school system and the government be fair to me, I also have to be fair to them.

There is a common code of ethics we must presume in one another if we are to live together at all. Even if the civil law did not make perjury a punishable crime, we have to count on the fact that when we give our word to one another—to tell the whole truth, to pay back a loan, to fix the sink—we really mean it on both sides. Even if the civil law did not make libel a punishable crime, we have to count on the fact that people are not spreading lies behind our backs or undermining our reputations—and they have to presume the same from us. Even if the civil law did not make theft and arson and murder and rape punishable crimes, in order to avoid madness we have to count on the fact that we will not wake up every morning to find all our possessions stolen and our houses burned to the ground, our sons murdered and our daughters raped.

Our fury at those crimes presumes a norm of legitimate human behavior, no matter what our particular government says. Our fury has nothing to do with the fact that there's a law against those actions in this paticular society and that people have broken that law. Our fury comes from the fact that the criminal had no *right*—even if he had on a police uniform and a court order in his hand—to harm me that way. On the contrary, *I* have a right to my possessions, my house, my sons and my daughters. The United States Constitution does not give me those rights. On the contrary, it says very clearly that all men and women are "endowed by their Creator," not by any particular government, with rights that are "inalienable"—not because we are Americans but because we are human. And my fury against the violation of those rights will be just as violent and as justified as the fury of a cave man or a desert nomad or a Mayan serf. Times—and man's nature—have not changed *that* much!

Those actions were anti-human and, therefore, wrong long before the civil law made them punishable. They were wrong even before the Judaic Commandments spelled them out. They were sinful because they violated the human nature not only of the victim but of the criminal. Anyone who robs me or burns me or rapes me lessens me as a human being by treating me as less human than himself, and in so doing also lessens himself as a human being. He has turned me into a sheep and himself into a wolf.

Furthermore, if one says that cheating on an exam is not even trivially "sinful," let him not get angry at being operated on by a doctor who has cheated his way through medical school. You are both in the same game; he just has bigger opportunities than you have—and more guts. If one says morality is judged by the situation and that only the individual can judge in any particular set of unique circumstances whether he is in fact dispensed from "the moral law," let him not get angry at the Watergate conspirators. That's precisely what they did, and their only fault was that they were caught by a group who, arbitrarily, thought differently. If one says that aborting babies in America is perfectly moral, let him not say that dropping bombs in Indochina is immoral. In both cases there is exactly the same chance that you will kill—or not kill—something human. If one says that morality is something that varies from society to society, let him not get angry if a new Hitler arises and annihilates another seven million Jews. At the time, Hitler *was* the law of his society, and his society said killing Jews was good and, therefore, according to the principle, it was a positively moral act. We have no more than a difference of opinion with him and his society. Hitler's only fault was that he lost World War II—a war, according to the principle, unjustly waged against him in an imperialist attempt to impose *our* society's idea of Jews on his society's idea of them.

Again, I suspect an ulterior motive here too. If one can convince himself that the world and man have so radically changed, he can argue that his parents and grandparents have nothing to offer him in his personal struggles to discover what is good and evil in this present world. All their warnings and regulations have no basis in this utterly changed world. But anyone who says that the nature of man is a myth, an idea whose objective content varies substantially from society to society and from generation to generation, betrays several other ignorances springing from those secondary roots.

First of all, he shows an ignorance of the difference between objective reality and subjective *awareness* of that reality. Just as babies are objectively male or female without their knowing it, just as colors exist objectively even though blind people are unaware of them, so also murdering female babies can be evil even if the Chinese acted otherwise, and mercy killing the retarded can be evil even if the Nazis acted otherwise. I think that too often in our moral discussions we focus our attention on the guilt of the perpetrator and not on the loss of the victim. Whether the child killer or the mercy killer subjectively acknowledges it or not, the victim has objectively lost something very real: his life. An evil thing has been done.

A second ignorance reveals itself in those who say man's nature changes radically—the ignorance of words. If man's nature is *so* different now from what it was in 1920 or 1820 or 20 B.C., that our fathers' code of right and wrong has no bearing on our own, then we cannot even *use* the word "man." If man changes so substantially as a moral being, then there is no such thing as evolution; instead, there is a mere substitution every generation or so of a completely new and unrelated "thing." Manifestly absurd as that is, it is the unavoidable logical conclusion for those who claim that "what was right or wrong for one generation is not necessarily right or wrong for this generation."

Of course customs and manners and styles change from generation to generation, and anyone with any sense of history at all can trace the recurring swing from conservatism to liberalism and back again. Skirts go up or down, hair gets longer or shorter, people hide their sexual activities or broadcast them without a blush. But we are talking here not of manners but of morals. The length of skirts *does* have something to do with sexuality, and the length of hair *does* have something to do with rebellion and independence, and talking openly about sex *does* make "mistakes" more frequent (or at least more obvious) than hushing them up.

The need for sex and independence have been around for a long time, and the question was never *whether* they were right or wrong but *when* they were right or wrong. There will probably be just as

many broken hearts and broken persons whether
skirts or hair are long or short. But no matter what
the style or time, the real question is: when is it right
to take the risk of breaking hearts or persons?

A third ignorance, one related to the former two
and one that feeds them with even greater infusions
of ignorance, is the calculated ignorance of history
and literature. I suggest the cause for this may sound
trivial, but I think that practically, at the beginning,
the cause is a student saying to himself: "That reading is so much work. If I can convince myself that it
has nothing really to tell me about living my life, I
won't have to study it. Just memorize the dates and
pass the exam." And so, started on the way by this
practical decision and encouraged by inertia, he need
never burden himself with the lessons of the past. If
one knows nothing at all about 500 B.C., one can
say that the morals of 500 B.C. were totally unlike
our own—right? Sheltered in the Seventies, we can
insulate ourselves from any of the bothersome sug-
gestions of Socrates or Jesus Christ or Abe Lincoln
or Mohandas Ghandi. They just don't experience *our*
world of *Playboy* and urbanization and atom bombs.
As if Socrates and Jesus and Lincoln and Ghandi
had no experience of sex, or loneliness in the crowd,
or fear of death; as if they wrestled with a sexuality,
or a loneliness, or a death far different from our own
today.

Oddly, I just realized that the four men I had
honestly picked at random as I wrote were all assassinated. And the one I had thought of adding from

recent history who might still be a source of meaning
was Jack Kennedy. If they were assassinated, they
must have lived "importantly" enough to have been
visible, make enemies, court danger. Far safer to
remain ignorant of their ways because their ways led
to death—as if death were the worst thing a man or
woman could suffer; as if smallness and ignorance
had ever staved off death.

Basically, I think, this objection to the reality of
personal sin rests on the ignorance that says that
laws and commandments make things evil—as if
such actions had not been evil before the laws were
framed or the commandments given. Surely, murdering one's brother was wrong for Cain even though
it took place long before Moses told the Israelites
that it was. Surely, kidnapping was evil long before
Bruno Hauptmann stole the Lindbergh baby and the
U.S. Congress made it a capital offense.

God knows the nature of human beings, how
they work, how they weakly dehumanize themselves.
So, because we were too dumb to profit from our
own experience and the natural consequences of
those sins, he asked a man to write them down so it
would be less easy to forget what made us less
human. Lawmakers, to a lesser degree and more
fallibly than God, also have experience of how
human beings act and how they dehumanize themselves and their neighbors. And so, after certain re-
currences of a particular dehumanizing act, they
pass a law against it—not to make it a sin (being
inhuman already did that) but to go further and

make it a crime, with a specific, this-world punishment.

I admit that pharisaeism—the picky-picky idolatry of the law, the conviction that the law makes all violators always interiorly guilty, the scrupulous adherence to the letter without mercy or love—is itself a perversion of human nature. But in legitimately rejecting such a dehumanizing perversion, many run blindly in the opposite direction to the denial of any possibility of sin or guilt or responsibility. And, in effect, to an opposite but equally deadly dehumanization.

Socialization Causes Guilt

An argument against the possibility of the existence of sin has grown as a result of the increasing visibility of the behaviorist psychology of Dr. B.F. Skinner. For the loftiest of motives and with impressive results, Skinner projects a method of education (and therefore of looking at the nature of human beings) that, by reinforcing "good" actions, hopes to eliminate antisocial behavior and therefore rid the streets of crime and the world of war.

The supposition of this theory is that any individual is merely a conglomerate of his previous programming and socialization: his genes, ethnic stereotype, treatment by parents, neighborhood, education. To a certain degree, no one can deny that we are very much "formed" in our values, attitudes and

judgments by the propaganda we have been force-
fed. Furthermore, the apparatus of behaviorist rein-
forcement has a great deal to recommend it educa-
tionally.

But I have great difficulty with this view of
what a man is. For one thing, who is to say what's
"good" and therefore to be reinforced? Dr. Skinner's
values are, as far as I can see, quite laudable, but his
apparatus could be (and in a clumsy way already is)
used just as well by the Mafia, the Red Chinese and
the American Nazi Party. Effectiveness is no guarantee of truth or goodness, as is evidenced by Nero,
bubonic plague and Hiroshima.

More importantly, if a man is and always has
been enslaved *totally* and *exclusively* to the values of
his programers and socializers, how is it that one
sees so much rebellion against those very propagan-
dists: parents, schools, society? Was their propaganda merely inefficient? If so, do the future programers
merely eliminate contact with altenative ideas; for
example, if the Chief Programer is a conservative,
will we burn all the liberal books? In asking us to
surrender the outmoded and divisive ideas of both
freedom and dignity, Dr. Skinner is also making us
surrender diversity of ideas and opinions. What a
dull world it will be, whether the only books are Dr.
Skinner's books or Chairman Mao's little red one.
What would it be like at a cocktail party, a class or a
TV talk show if everybody had the same ideas?

C.S. Lewis says that the future eugenist who de-
termines biologically who will be allowed to live will

be the Ultimate Slaver. He will control what eye colors and nose sizes and torsos are "right." But even more enslaving will be the Ultimate Behaviorist who can determine what ideas and values are "right" and can train all men and women so that they are no longer free to "break" the rules. (You thought the Ten Commandments were bad!)

When Dr. Skinner comes into his kingdom, where freedom and, therfore, sin no longer exist, there will be no more Shakespeare. No play or novel can be written when men are not free to make intriguing mistakes and to wrest their dignity from opposition and from their own weakness. It is with scrupulous honesty that Dr. Skinner calls his masterwork *Beyond Freedom and Dignity*. He recognizes that, inevitably, the total elimination of antisocial behavior necessarily entails the surrender of freedom (all totalitarians have recognized the same thing). But the surrender of freedom to even the most benevolent programer necessarily means the surrender of one's personal dignity. If the programer takes the responsibility for eliminating all blameworthy actions of his "subjects," he also takes the credit for any praiseworthy action of his subjects. The subject is not good; he is merely unbad. It will not be "I" who succeed; it will be my programer who succeeds. Granted that in Skinner's paradise there would be no "sin" (meaning antisocial behavior), but neither would there be any prizes. Not only will there be no Shakespeare; there will be no football games.

I often wonder if my students, who seem to accept Dr. Skinner's vision of man so uncritically, real-

ly understand the price he is very forthrightly asking
for the comfort of living in a sinless world. Granted
that one jettisons with a single heave all the guilt for
one's mistakes and selfishness and even cruelty by
laying the guilt to faulty programing. ("How can
you expect me to act any differently when I've been
socialized in a society like this, with old-fashioned
parents and teachers like mine!") But the price for
that carefree irresponsibility is precisely the two
prizes all young people crave so desperately—the
freedom to choose who *I* want to be and the dignity
of being respected for who I have made myself. Here
is calculated ignorance at its best: "I can make my
own decisions!" coming from the same mouth that
says: "All men's decisions come from their programing!"

If nothing I do is sinful—or if any "fault" is at
least understandable and therefore immediately for-
gettable—then nothing I do is important. My self—
like my actions—is as negligible as the indiscrim-
inate ruttings of a bull. If, on the other hand, my
"bad" actions are capable of rupturing my relationship with an infinite, eternal and all-loving Father, I am one very important cat indeed!

Claiming to be a person worth respect without
claiming the responsibility for one's own actions is
as impossible as claiming sanctity without the freedom to be a sinner. When one surrenders responsibility for one's actions, he surrenders not only the responsibility for his "bad" actions but also for his
good actions. Moreover, he surrenders his claim to
freedom. He surrenders his human dignity as well,

which can be forged only by getting up when he's fallen, acknowledging his mistake with honesty rather than with self-defensive alibis, and consciously overcoming the fall.

The surrender of all of that is a very high price to pay for conscience-free comfort.

As Long as You Hurt Only Yourself

Even one who will admit actual sinfulness in hurting others will often draw the line where the so-called sin affects only himself: smoking dope, masturbation, alcoholism, self-imposed ignorance and the like. The argument is: "If there are any negative consequences, I am the only one who will suffer them."

This is true only in the sense that the perpetrator and the victim are the same person. But the consequences are not restricted there. Presumably there are people who love the perpetrator-victim and, whether he likes it or not, his self-destruction is a violence to them, and his self-diminishing impoverishes them too. What's more, there are untold lives that could have been enriched by this lessened life and will never be. It is a sin of omission rather than commission, and yet other human lives are lessened by it. No man is an island; in impoverishing myself I impoverish everyone I will ever meet thereafter. Carson McCullers has said that the heart of a self-centered and self-sufficient person grows smaller and harder with each bit of self-degradation until it is as small and pitted as the seed of a peach. Every selfishness, even one known only to me, makes me less free to forget myself and to grow less full than I could have been and less able to love.

Those who profess this point of view argue further that if someone is engaged in some action harmful only to himself, no one has the right to interfere. This argument seems to me as moronic as saying that, if someone is attempting suicide, one has no right to interfere and try to convince him to live.

What You Don't Acknowledge Doesn't Exist

Another attempt to negate the consequences of sin, even when its actuality is admitted, is trivial, but I include it here simply because I have heard it too often to hope that its stupidity is guarantee enough that no one is so ignorant as to hold it.

The argument goes something like this: "If I don't *feel* sinful, then I haven't sinned, right? I remember them saying in grammar school that if you don't *know* it's a sin, then it's not a sin, right? Therefore, the less you know, the less you can sin. Right?" Right. Cows and apes and mountain lions never sin, only humans can. The question is whether you are one of those.

I suspect it is foolish for me to include such a self-deceiving argument because if you have read this

far you are intelligent enough to see how pitifully
self-demeaning it is.

All right, then, suppose I admit that man does
—through his own responsibility and fault, perhaps
rarely but truly—commit real sin. What does "sin"
mean? Surely you're not going to give us that mortal-venial stuff and the old simplistic stories about
going to hell for the only mortal sin you ever com-
mitted no matter how good the rest of your life was!

No. I'm not.

The Meaning of Sin

I begin with the premise that, by their very
make-up, human beings differ from beasts. They are
able to think and reflect; they are able freely to
choose, with at least some knowledge of the possible
consequences of their choices and actions. Further,
my own experience and the experiences other men
and women have shared with me personally and in
books and films convince me that the one thing that
fulfills a man or woman is love—the unselfish giving
of oneself to another, without any necessary kick-
backs to oneself, even at a sacrifice to oneself. There
is no human being who doesn't need love; there is no
one utterly incapable of giving love. But without love
—or with very little of it given and received—a man
or woman or child is starved more completely than
he or she would be with little or no material food.
On the other hand, if one does have the unalterable

conviction that one loves and is loved, he or she can survive almost anything. Even death. Dachau alone is proof enough of that.

I am further convinced that love not only enables a human being to survive; love makes him or her grow precisely *as* a human being.

From these premises, which seem to me to be undeniable, I am left with the conclusion that growing in ability to know and love is what human beings are "for." Therefore, anything that promotes the ability to know and love is good; anything that inhibits that ability is evil—that is, sin. I am not using sin in the old-time pattern of images where a vengeful God sits at a desk like some ink-stained Dickensian clerk, watching every move, totting up the balance sheets. I am not speaking in the images of the sinner's soul as a soiled garment or a dirty milk bottle or a sodden Brillo pad. I am speaking in terms of a human being less and less able to love with the full potential of love he or she is capable of.

Those actions are sinful that almost invariably dehumanize me, turn me inward to the animal law of self-preservation rather than outward to the human law of self-transcendence. In some cases, one feels the impulse (call it "grace" if you will) to be generous, and yet he draws back, preferring safe ungrowth to risky growth. Or in other cases, one feels drawn downward and inward, unwilling or too fearful to act like a human being who foresees the consequences of his actions to himself and others he claims to love— and he follows that demeaning call to retreat. That, I think, is sin.

There are trivial withdrawals from growth, and serious withdrawals and deadly withdrawals. Perhaps the only way I personally can understand it is by a comparison to marriage love. A husband has a few nasty habits his wife finds distasteful; they're real faults and, if he loves her, he'll try to eliminate them, but they're hardly a threat to their love relationship. These are like what we were always used to calling "venial sins."

But there are more serious withdrawals. The husband plays around. Let's say he sleeps a few times with his secretary or a neighbor. If he and his wife truly love one another, they can work it out with a great deal of understanding and sacrifice on both sides, and the relationship is often all the stronger afterward because of that shared giving. But it is serious, a threat to the relationship that's not going to be cured by the husband's saying, "Oh, she'll never find out," or "Dammit! That was stupid, moronic, unkind—but I'd better forget it or I'll suffer guilt feelings." In the old black-white, mortal-venial setup of the catechism, there was no category corresponding to the "serious sin" that is short of mortal but far heavier than venial. And I think the catechism's attempt to be so hard-and-fast has ruined many a good person's respect for real sin— and therefore for himself. If any sin more serious than trivial sin is *ipso facto* mortal, then what hope has a man or woman with ordinary human weaknesses? After all, it is a dogma of the Church that no man or woman without some special grace can long avoid serious sin. It's the way we're made. But if every serious sin is mortal, deadly, completely destructive of the relationship with God, we might as well all give up. And many do.

Deadly withdrawals are far less frequent than the catechism made us believe as susceptible kids, because such a sin is usually the *terminal* withdrawal at the end of a long line of serious withdrawals. In the analogy, the husband has insulted his relationship with his wife so often, with such increasing regularity and seriousness, that the relationship of love between them has died and only a total change on his part can set things on the road to being right again. If such a setting-right comes about, it is a "resurrection from the dead," like the one beautifully pictured in the parable of the prodigal son. But if the relationship cannot be set right, then somewhere along the line the relationship has died.

In a true love relationship, there is no "How far can I go?" As soon as someone asks: "How far can I cheat before she can't possibly love me anymore?" he has already stopped loving. At least from his point of view, the relationship is already dead.

There is no point, no hard-and-fast line where one action in a string of serious sins can be predicted to be *the* deadly sin, the ultimate straw that crumples the camel. One can see love dying; one can see when it is dead. But there is no moment, no particular betrayal of love, when he can say: "This is the one."

Real sin—serious or deadly—is not just being

caught in a mistake and kicking oneself for being so stupid. There is an inner need to apologize; there is the conviction of failure at the deepest level of one's personhood.

Accepting the reality of sinfulness is not accepting a life of perpetual self-examination or a life of endlessly crippling guilt feelings. If one feels guilty beyond the cause of his guilt or with no cause for guilt at all, a psychiatrist is savior enough for him. Nor does accepting the reality of one's sinfulness mean that such a person is bad, rotten to the core. If that were so, there would be no hope of salvation, no life left to rebuild on. A thoroughly bad person would, by definition, never ask to be saved because he would be absolutely incapable of any guilt feelings at all! Ironically, guilt feelings over a truly serious offense are a sure sign that the person is still good enough to acknowledge his error.

Accepting the reality of sin is accepting two facts that seem indisputable to most reflective people: "The good that I want to do, I don't do; the evil that I don't want to do, I do." It is a *good* man or woman who acknowledges that they have an inertia to the growth of unselfishness and love and a heavy gravitation to the comfort of sterile self-protectiveness and self-service.

The consequent need to apologize and be forgiven (the need for "salvation" and "resurrection") is really not so much for the sake of the beloved whom we have made a victim; if the beloved had stopped loving the perpetrator, there would be no hope either of apology or of salvation. The need to apologize is on the part of the perpetrator: to set things right, to make things whole again at the deepest level of his own personhood. It is an honest admission and forthright confession of his selfishness in order that he may be healed by love and be able to grow in love once more.

Unbelief

This chapter has dealt with the ways calculated ignorance denies sin—by saying morality today is utterly different from morality yesterday, by saying mistakes come from programing, by admitting injustice against others but not against myself, by pretending I don't know.

But what has this to do with unbelief. Simple. "If I haven't done any evil, there's no need to apologize, right? And the only reason that the idea of God was invented was to keep us in line, keep us guilty, keep us scared, right? But if there's no reason to feel guilty about anything I do, then there's no reason for God, right? Therefore, God doesn't exist. Right?"

Wrong. But just try to explain *why* it's wrong to someone whose self-protectiveness has locked his mind so tightly that no contrary ideas can get in any more. Basically, I think the reason for this self-deception is that apologies are embarrassing. The saddest result of this stance is not just the rejection of the obvious fact of evil in oneself or the pitiably stupid pretense at logic on which the rejection is based. The saddest result is the small, smug, childishly selfish lives that grow stuntedly out of such self-delusion. To avoid an occasional honest admission of stupidity, one rejects responsibility for his own actions and therefore rejects the fulfillment of his self. To avoid the momentary embarrassment of an apology, one rejects the God who is not only the receiver of the apology but the giver of forgiveness, of love, of new life.

If you never feel guilt, then you have no need of a Savior who transcends not only time and space but weakness and failure. You have no need of the Jesus who ransomed mankind on a criminal's cross. You have no need for the father of the prodigal son.

Till your self-delusions run out.

4. IGNORANT CONTENTMENT WITH A FALSE GOD

In the Old Testament, the best way to lure the old Israelites away from Yahweh was to whip up a new and intriguing idolatry that specialized in temple prostitution, lots of big gongs and bells, plenty of food and booze. And if you could haul in a golden calf as well you were home free. Hollywood, for all its self-serving prudery, does it very well. Hugh Hefner and Madison Avenue do it even better.

Poor Hugh Hefner! He and his magazines have become, with his own willing connivance, the symbol of sexual and "artistic" and gustatory and financial liberation. He has become what Nero was for earlier centuries: a worldly wise man shrewd enough to realize that when the whole world is burning down around your ears the only sensible thing to do is to fiddle around.

Poor old Madison Avenue! The admen have to make a living, and it is ungrateful of us not to thank them for keeping the rivers of money sluicing into the Divine Economy and out to the helplessly thirsty jobhunters and consumers. At whatever price, the Economy must have its sacrifices or we will all die— even at the price of lies, even at the price of false promises, even at the price of the bastardization of Christmas and of giving thanks to God and mother and young love and marriage and death and the Resurrection. Each one exists primarily to sell: cards, flowers, gifts, whatever. The Economy must be fed even at the price of building false expectations of life and frustrated self-distaste into the young warriors and virgins of the tribe, for whom every new pimple is one more contrast between their unworthy selves and the beautifully ideal people in the commercials. The poor admen have become what the Sirens were for earlier centuries: beautiful singers luring men to their deaths with beautiful songs.

But let's not put all the blame on poor old Hugh and the admen. Mr. Hefner does not publish his magazines from some apostolic notion like liberating us from the darkness of our Puritan hangups— though that is the motive he claims. He publishes them because they sell and because whatever sells not only makes money at the magazine racks but also sells ad space. And admen are not wearing themselves out to make the world a happier place; they are working to make money, and one makes money by giving people what they want. No one continues to offer a magazine or a product for sale when no one wants to buy. The *Playboy* Philosopher and the advertising hucksters don't make us what we are; they merely supply the means for us to make ourselves more what we already want to be. As with the Israelites in the desert, the golden bull in the hand is worth two Promised Lands in the bush.

If Hugh and the admen thought that the consumers were *really* hungry for clear water and healthy Biafrans and were willing to pay for it, they'd sell that.

If what follows sounds cynical and savage, it was intended to be. The Law of the American Dream is more subtle in its statements and more sophisticated in its methods and goals than the Law of the Jungle, but it is no less savage.

Many, many years ago, the guidebook of the "Century of Progress Exhibition" stated the materialism of the American Dream with admirable forthrightness: "Science discovers, genius invents, industry applies. And man adapts himself to, or is molded by, new things."

We are not in control of who we are or become; "they" are. Blunt, but very close, I think, to the way things have worked out.

We are, most of us, idolaters in thrall to the Economy—which is to say, in an indirect way, to our own self-interests. Our freely chosen and subsidized priests are the scientists and artisans who answer our prayers for more and more ease and pampering. It is the advertisers and the Hefners who call us to even further greed, and therefore to greater devoted petitions for more goods and services. And, according to the limits of the game, we all benefit: the harder you work, the more money you have to spend; the more money you have to spend, the more the Economy thrives; the more the Economy thrives, the more money you have to spend; the more money. . . .

And so it goes.

If it sounds a bit closed, a bit stifling, a bit circular, it's because most squirrel cages are.

Besides priests, there are also highly sophisticated scriptures in the comfortable idolatry: for the upper levels—the hierarchy—there are *Fortune* and *Business Week*; for the lower levels—the faithful— there are *People* and *Foxylady*. And for all levels, there are the audiovisual "scriptures" proclaiming the good news everywhere, heralds of the liberating truth before whose variety the power to describe stands speechless. Where can you go without seeing or hearing the message of the Idol, which is: Buy! Subways, taxis, buses, elevators, your own breakfast table? On top of buildings, along every highway, in the sky! In your own living room every ten minutes; at your ear in the transistors every three minutes!

"Aw, nobody pays attention to ads. We're all wise to that!"

If that's so, then those dumb corporations are sure wasting a lot of billions every year pushing those deodorants! *Somebody* down here must love them.

The one real sin against the Idol, his priests and his scriptures is taking time to think, time to look at alternatives, time to criticize. Don't you bother thinking; we'll do that for you. And the Idol's defense against thinking is not unlike the drills military recruits were forced to undergo hour after hour. Now, no modern army marches into battle in lines and columns any more and yet, for what seemed like an eternity, men snapped "Left! Right! To the rear!" And the purpose was that they should have no time to think when an order was given later on. When the lieutenant in battle says, "Okay, men! We may have 70% casualties in this caper, but we've gotta take Porkchop Hill! Move out!"—no one balks. Hopefully. If anyone stopped to think, to look at alternatives, to criticize, he might say: "Now wait just a minute! Is this acre or two of rock worth the one life I'll ever have? For 'a piece of land not big enough to bury the dead'?" What would happen to war then?

The admen use the same methods as the drill sergeant. All those smothering challenges to "better, newer, improved, bigger, livelier" lives which these products are going to lead us to, challenges that come firing out of every medium at us all day long— have the same purpose as the unrelenting drills: Don't give 'em time to think. And, although the names and promises and the orders-to-buy are as innumerable and varied as the stars, without fail the message of every one is exactly the same: "THE MORE THINGS YOU HAVE, THE HAPPIER YOU'LL BE!"

But no drill sergeant, no voodoo hypnotist, no Siberian brainwasher ever had such omnipresence, such compliant subjects, or such sophisticated and successful methods as the huckster-priests of the Idol —the Economy. And we don't mind, really. After all, it's good for all of us. It's a very thorough evangelization.

The moral code of the idolatry is strict: work, compete. Not that it is ever stated that openly and intimidatingly. One merely needs to create a ravening need within the "subjects" and convince them that only with money will they fulfill that need, and they'll work, beg, borrow or steal forever to satisfy their "habit." It is savage, but subtle. Even the name of the Idol, "Economy," has been deftly turned around so that it no longer means what it used to: care in buying, conserving, frugality, thrift. It now means expansion, spending, the bullish market. All of these changes are very subtle so that most of the work goes on inside the "subject," in that dark place inside where he says: "I want."

From the time they are able to stare at the Electronic Babysitter, the promising little consumers hear the quiet little challenge to hunger under the loud noises and colors: "The more things you have, the happier you'll be, isn't that right? You don't want to be like those *poor* children, *do* you? They have acne and bad breath and underarm stains. They don't have a nice car or a place in the country or Barbie Dolls. Let's see if we can't convince Daddy and Mommy to work just a little harder, all right, so we can have more things? And then you'll be *loved*."

Simultaneously, all the knowing and unknowing votaries of the system are helping to nurture and purify this desire for goods and services, for further competition: sibling rivalries, parental expectations, report cards, College Board scores, who's invited to the prom, who wins the raffle drive, who's got more lines in the yearbook or the play, who plays quarterback, who can buy more pagan babies? Compete! Compete! And they listen. And they learn what's important.

As in any other religion, there are many virtues of the Idol that must be celebrated, but among the greatest is proving one's value by efficiency and speed, until efficiency and speed become demigods unto themselves. In the old days, men and women made something and also sold it, and most often to neighbors whom they cared about. Not only did such people feel responsible for the quality of what they made, but the care they took in the making made them proud of their work and their lives.

But since Henry Ford invented the more efficient, speedier assembly line, men and women see only a part of the whole product and, anonymously, they plug in this part or solder that plate or paint a thing that a hundred other faceless hands have put together. They do not put their names on what they do, no stamp of themselves. It is not theirs and they do not know to whom it will be sold; why should they care if it is only "good enough"? The sooner it breaks down, the sooner the purchaser will have to buy another. Shoddy work is good for the Economy, and the Economy is good for all of us.

Martin Luther King once said: "If your job is to sweep streets, sweep those streets the way Michelangelo would have swept streets." It will come as no great revelation to anyone that there is not much of *that* going around nowadays.

But the idolatry is not that unrelievedly grim and puritanical. There are also celebrations! Great multitudes of people enthusiastically celebrating competition! And if one can't actually be present at the competitive services himself, he can always watch them at home. There are elections (where the candidates are polished and packaged and purged of impurities, like detergents). There are summit meetings (where human beings are used as bargaining counters for land and oil and "spheres of influence"). There are the annual Academy Awards and Emmys and Tonys and Grammys and Miss Anything (where probing the human spirit yields to probing of the human pocketbook). But most accessibly, there is the wide world of sports (where the champions command salaries that show social workers what fools they are). And, above all, there is the mating game (where one takes to the dance not a person but a companion body by which others will judge him, where success is so often measured by the degree of "what I got off her," where bodies couple in search of something more than flesh).

And High Priest Hefner smiles benignly. How well it has all worked. It's all very beautiful.

As in all idolatries, even the idolatry of Big Brother in *1984*, there must be a publicized enemy who is really in league with the Idol. For the secular Idol it is the much publicized, much warned-against counter culture, with its rock music, funky clothes and drugs.

How gullible—or devoted—we must be not to stop and realize that it is the big corporations who sell the "underground" records and pay enormous salaries to the "nonconformist" artists who produce them. How loyal we are not to notice that our funky uniforms of jeans and flannel shirts have Sears-Roebuck labels. How compliant we are, not to recognize that it is the *Organization* that sells the dope with which we prove our nonconformity to the organized system.

Love is blind.

There is one heresy for the idolater: unblindness —not just-pretend unblindness, not just cocktail party sophistication, but real thinking, real challenging. That is a threat to the jobs of the Idol's priests, a threat to turn even the contented worshippers out of the temple.

Wisely, such a threatening heresy is handled as all heresies should be handled: by ignoring it. Or, if that won't work, by making it look silly: popularizing moron-priests like the one on *M*A*S*H*, caricaturing eggheads, making the cautious look cowardly. Further, by making the music so much louder, the billboards so much bigger, the football games so much more frequent, the scandals so much juicier— they assure themselves that no one can hear the voice of one crying in the wilderness.

As I have described it, this all sounds like a conspiracy, and in a sense it is. But it is not manipulated by a group of financiers with code names and secret meeting places; it is merely the result of the welcomed emergence and deification of many of the worst aspects of human beings—vices we all share: greed, lust, gluttony, envy—in a word, self-serving interests. No lioness feels compunction or makes apologies to the gazelle when she falls on it and tears it to pieces. The gazelle is a means; the lioness and her cubs come first. This is too often the same sanctified dehumanization employed by the Idol, Economy, and her prophets—business, government, international politics: "T'hell with the others. What's in it for *our* side?"

The Idol's Enemy

But what do materialism and competition have to do with the roots of religious unbelief? Well, against such ominpresence, such efficiency at hypnotism, such immediate reward with money-back guarantees, is it any wonder our churches and seminaries and convents are dwindling?

By now, the Idol's opposition is so unappealing to the man who has been bribed into limiting himself to a body and a mind that it can very easily be ignored.

Instead of a tangible god who promises immediate, provable satisfaction here and now, religion has a God who promises invisible, intangible spiritual growth, now and forever. But one has to take all those promises on trust. Whereas the Idol can be hauled into court and sued for malfeasance, religion offers a God who remains—for his own reasons—too often aloof and silent, answerable to no man.

Instead of priests who "know where it's at, know what we really want," religion offers priests who are often as confused as the people they serve.

Whereas the priests and prophets of the Idol make a concerted effort to offer concrete means to cover up one's deficiencies quickly and visibly with big cars and soothing creams, religion offers priests who ask for one's honest confrontation with his true self, forthright admission of his weakness and an inner resolution that he is precious enough to undergo change.

Instead of scriptures that embody the message of selfishness as a virtue, so desirably, so omnipresently, so apparently justifiably, religion has an old-fashioned book couched in terms no one can understand, and a message that is very hard indeed. Whereas the message of the Idol is: "We're Number One!" religion offers a ragged rabbi who got nowhere himself, who died for his beliefs and his brethren, and whose battle cry is: "If you will be first, be last; if you will rule, then serve." Sunday Mass will never outdraw Monday-night football!

Instead of an appealing moral code that says "Anything goes!" as long as it doesn't mess up the Economy, a code that has given us moon landings and the automobile and the greatest (or at least the largest) school system in history, religion offers caution, prayer, surrender of one's own desires to the needs of others. It demands that we love those in need, indiscriminately—which is manifestly foolish, right?

Instead of celebrations of competitions where tens of thousands cheer, religion offers a table with ordinary dull bread and wine.

If the key to happiness is truly having more tangible things, if the greatest wisdom is taking care of oneself and one's own—and the rest be damned, if one's bank balance is the index of his true value, then religion asks too much and gives too little.

What's in it for me? Where are the results? What's it really *worth*?

"Is that all there is, my friend? Then keep on dancing. Let's break out the booze!"

If you are content with this answer and all its works and all its pomps, you surely will feel no need for a Savior.

Till the money runs out.

5. IGNORANCE
   OF DEATH

Most people pray only when they feel small.

That's why it's so easy to pray by the ocean. It is so vast and imperturbable, and we by contrast are so diminished and transitory. It's easier to pray when the sky is ablaze with stars, or in a foxhole during a battle, or when one's made a fool of himself, or sinned. We feel small, dependent and utterly alone on an unbright cinder spinning through the endless cold of space. Like children alone in the dark, we cry for our Father.

Of course, we *are* small all the time. It's only when reality breaks through our defenses against it that we *feel* small. And then we pray.

At other times—most times—we defend ourselves with shields we have forged over the years against the truth of our cosmic smallness: the sales records, the false eyelashes, the euchre games, the necking. "See! I am not alone. I am important, independent. A big shot."

If we were ever to see our paltry seventy-year lives set against the indisputable and nearly endless line of time stretching backward through the four thousand years of recorded human history and

beyond, through the millions of years since the settling of this planet in orbit, and beyond that, again,
along the limitless chain of years that the universe
has been here, we would feel very small indeed.

Or if we could try to see ourselves against the
objective and undeniable enormity of space, trying to
pinpoint "me" as an infinitesimal speck against the
background of this solar system and the countless
solar systems of the universe, we would feel very
small indeed.

Or if we could pile our human accomplishments
—the good deeds, the creations, the children—
against the background of the accumulated accomplishments of the entire human race since our
beginning: the conquests of Alexander and Caesar,
the wisdom of Solomon and Einstein, the courage of
Helen Keller and Martin Luther King, the art of da
Vinci and Picasso, the sheer number of children of
all mankind, or even merely of modern China—we
would feel very small indeed.

But we choose not to see ourselves as small. Even
when we are.

And yet, compared to the endless years of cosmic time, my seventy years (if I have that many) are
negligible; compared to the vast wastes of space, the
area my body takes up is negligible, compared to the
triumphs and depravities of all human history, my
successes and my sins are negligible.

These three backgrounds are facts—objective
and indisputable—and the conclusions regarding my
negligibility are equally unarguable. Unarguable, but
not unavoidable. They are disturbing facts but, once

again, calculated ignorance of them can "save" me. So, I focus down to this planet, this country, to my neighborhood or tract or backyard. I build hedges, mow the lawn, worry about my marks and my salary —manageable problems. I form a tiny protective circle of trusted friends, and can therefore forget the anonymous faces in the subway, and even more the faceless nobodies in Palestine refugee camps and the streets of Calcutta and, certainly, the faceless God "out there somewhere." From behind my hedges they look no more intimidating to me than the remotest stars.

As we have seen before, though, God or nature or *Some*body refuses to allow for too long this self-blinding to the truth, this embedding in the comfortably self-delusive womb. Sooner or later there's going to be those unpleasant contractions of the womb—and that painful slap. And the two weapons of rebirth are the encounter with suffering and the encounter with death.

Suffering

No one is safe from suffering. You are never too young or too old. You are never so rich that you can bribe it away; you are never so poor that you can hope it will finally have pity on you. Young or old, rich or poor, we are all greeted into this world by a slap on the butt. And it is the first of many. Sufferings dot the progress of our lives like milestones along a road. As children, we suffer them dully, waiting for Mommy or the doctor or God to take them away. But in adolescence, when we become more aware that we are reflective persons and that others are persons too, we begin to ask why, not just; "Why do I hurt now, Mommy?" but; "Why does anybody hurt, anytime? What have we done to deserve this?"

And of course if there is no God, there is no reason, anywhere, for anybody. That's just the way things are, kid. Tough.

Before adolescence, one is sheltered by childish incomprehension and by his parents' cautious protection from the ceaseless sufferings that blanket the world. Children watch the TV reportage of rapes, carnage, destruction and cannot tell the difference from war movies. We know nothing of Mommy's menstrual problems or Daddy's precarious finances. If one of the parents is a drunk or philanderer, we never know the cause of our pain, but merely suffer it mutely, like puppies in an incomprehensible thunderstorm. But in adolescence, when we know that we are as much persons as our parents and at least vaguely suspect that they are as much persons as we, and when we know at least viscerally that persons have *rights*, that they cannot be punished unless they've done something wrong, and when we compare the haves and the have-nots, the heroes and ourselves, the whole thing seems just too unfair. And we want to know why.

That pain over the inequity of things—when puberty forces us unwillingly to leave the womb of childhood—is the slap that makes us breathe the stronger air of human adulthood.

Thereafter, the sufferings are varied for each individual—hopes dashed, love unreturned or gone stale, talents unfulfilled or refused due attention, weaknesses unconquerable, intentions misunderstood —the list and its variants are interminable. The manifestations of sufferings in one's life may be large or small, bunched together at times and spaced out at others, but there is one thing sure: suffering is unavoidable.

It is in some sense a measure of one's achievement of adulthood that he or she can cope with adversity without dodging or even deserting. The fully-realized man or woman can face the worst life has— with no less pain than the fool, but with level-headedness, self-possession and the calm certainty that he or she will endure. In conquering adversity and suffering, one achieves his unique personal dignity. Unfortunately, many today evade any confrontation with even the idea of suffering as adamantly as they evade the solitude and silence and reflection that turn suffering into food for the spirit. And, oddly, they nonetheless wonder why they feel so inconsequential, so dispirited, so without dignity.

Suffering is, even for the wise atheist, the perplexing savior offering the chance to transcend a life of dull insignificance. In triumphing over sufferings great and small, men and women transcend *themselves*, live life in a stronger, higher key than their fellows who cower together in anonymous security.

Death

But there is one suffering no one—no matter how intrepid—can triumph over alone. No one can forever outwit death.

Other sufferings, deprivations or failures can be overcome with courage and wisdom and endurance. When they are past, one is filled with a sense of pride, relief and a deeper wisdom—like an athlete of the spirit who has qualified for even more difficult encounters.

But death is not something that "will pass and be over" if only one endures a bit longer. For the one dead, time has no meaning any more. The question is, however, whether the one dead also has no meaning any more.

Either death is a slap on the butt that wakes us into a new life, or it is merely a slap. The last one.

I am not saying that the one dead may not "live on" in his children, in his books, in his monuments. But it is a very pale and thin "living on" from the point of view of the one dead. *He* or *she* does not live on; something they made lives on, but they aren't there to know it. They aren't any "where." Very simply, they aren't. And eventually the children in their turn will die, the books become passé, the monuments crumble and fall to make way for someone else's monument. In any case, if the one dead at that final moment ceases to exist as a self-aware entity, *he* does not live on except as an idea, a memory that fades and in time is itself no more; *he* has ceased to be real.

It is a grisly prospect, and our inner selves, our spirits, rebel against it. We are more than willing to accept (even while we scrabble to pile it up) that we cannot carry money beyond the grave. As Thomas Hardy grimly puts it, money is too tough for the worms to chew. We know too that even the body and its brain, which can survive only on physical air, cannot long outlast its last breath and heartbeat. But here, at this unavoidable confrontation with the possibility of personal annihilation, we once again resurrect the hope that even if body and mind pass away, one thing *will* survive death: our spirits, our souls, our selves.

We have already seen in our lifetime how money and parts of the body and ideas can be lost, but *we*—whatever that means—can struggle on. The "I"—the treasury of joys, self-sacrifices, loves—*can* live beyond time because even when we were experiencing those "spiritual highs" we were somehow outside time and space, ungoverned by them.

Furthermore, it is the unshakable conviction of those who have grown used to prayer that again and again they have communicated with Someone who exists in a dimension free of time and space. Now, that seems improbable testimony to those who have never had such elevating experiences. Perhaps a comparison might help, though. If there were living beings on some other planet, we would have no way to be sure they were there—unless they sent us some decipherable communication. If such communications came regularly and understandably, with messages by which we could enrich our own lives, we would tend to believe not only that they were intelligent beings on that planet but that they were beings wiser than we are. And even though only a few experienced scientists were able to be at the complex devices of communication and to understand and translate these messages, after their conclusions had been publicized for a few months in the press and after countless people had begun to base their lives on the messages, with enriching results, we would tend to believe.

And yet, since recorded history began, that is precisely what people who are learned in prayer claim—not contact with beings somewhere else in space, but contact with a God who exists independent of time and space. For four thousand years they have published their findings, and men and women have listened and lived richer lives because of their messages.

Some can say that this type of communication is self-delusive, merely "voices in the head." But they are judging from the *outside*, from information the one praying can only inadequately supply about his experience in prayer. But the limitations of the critics' experience does not control or limit the extent and depth of the experience of the persons praying. We may have experienced Something, Someone they haven't met. We may know something they don't know—although they could.

What is it like, this "world" free of time and space and death? No one alive truly knows. Everything that we can even imagine about it is confined by the fact that our imaginations are stocked only with images of tangible, physical, this-world things and people and places. (We can't even describe love except in terms of physical heartbeats and physical skyrockets!) In older days, when the best life anyone could imagine was being the son of a king, the afterlife was pictured as a palace—with gates of pearl and streets of gold. But that was only the imagination's way of saying what it might be *like*. Is the description a photographic representation of what the afterlife is? No. Is the description a fumbling approximation of what it's going to *feel* like? In a way, yes.

In that way of existing—whatever it is like—there will be no "here and there"; there will be no "now and then." It will be awareness of self and the others—and the Other—so complete, so without misunderstanding, that it boggles minds that are themselves still incomplete and still misunderstand. It will be a fulfillment-to-overflowing of all that makes men and women human—sons and daughters of the Most High God. It will be Love.

Only one person has reputedly gone through the gates of death to this other way of existing and returned to tell it: Jesus Christ. We have only the word of those he spoke to that he did actually do it. But they died fearlessly, refusing to deny what Jesus had claimed or their personal experience of its results.

Because one has not been someplace, that doesn't mean it does not exist. I have never seen Katmandu, yet I trust that it is there. Because one cannot touch something, that doesn't mean it does not exist. I cannot touch love or honor or the inner spirits of my friends, yet I am as sure that they exist as I am that *I* exist.

Avoiding Death, Avoiding Life

Jesus' disciples wrote a book about how to enrich this present life with the realizations that, not only do we have our existence from a loving Father, not only can we be forgiven even for deadly breaks in our relationship with him, but that he will save us from death. Their book says that we can begin, at least in some pale way, to live in that other way of existing right here and now, from within space and time. And the key into that way of existing is this paradox: if you want to keep your life and enrich it, you must give it away.

That book, precisely because of that irritating paradox, is probably the most-bought and least-read book in the modern world. As any businessman or student or football player or general will tell you: losing is *not* the way to win.

It has become a contrapuntal refrain in this essay: the less you know, the safer you are from discomfort and from growth. And so the Gospels, with all their fiery challenges to a greater life than we'd planned, remain unread. In their place we content ourselves (sort of) with ignorable sermons about how to keep out of trouble and with holy pictures of an effeminate blasphemy, a toothless lion of Judah, who is not only not threatening but not even in much danger of becoming even interesting.

"I have come that you may have life—and have it more abundantly!"

This is just what we want to avoid.

Paradoxically, we avoid fuller life not only by negating the power of the Good News but by negating the power of death from which the Good News announces we can be freed. It surely has become obvious throughout that we have an infinite capacity to kid ourselves, and death—being the least desirable of realities—gets even more than its fair share of calculated cover-ups.

"Well, I have a long time before I have to face *that* reality!"

Sez who?

As much as possible, we treat death as the Victorians treated sex: Don't mention it in front of the children, shut it away behind the doors of hospitals and nursing homes and funeral parlors where it can be controlled. Or, using the opposite tack, treat it as a harmlessly sadistic staple of public entertainment in detective and spy shows, as it was in the Circus Maximus. Trivialize it or hide it, satirize it or ignore it. It will go away.

Further, nearly everything in American culture today conspires to make us forget the questions of aging and death. Even the persons we see dying before our very eyes on the evening news are called "casualties," not persons. And we cling to youthfulness even if it has to be faked with covering creams and dyes and ludicrous clothes, in the truly vain hope of avoiding death or at least the idea of it. Ignoring the idea of death is like dancing on the deck of the *Titanic* while the lifeboats hang there empty.

As a further shield against this intimidating truth, we have the Myth of Progress that encourages us to trust that, given enough time, all pain, disease, poverty, war and death will be eliminated.

And yet that's just the point. Who's "given enough time?"

Is it any wonder that to such self-deluded ears the whole concept of Jesus' resurrection sounds absolutely meaningless? It is like shouting about the beauty of color into the ears of a blind, deaf mute. How can anyone find any value in *resurrection* from death if he has never confronted and accepted the reality of *death*?

And of course if all your life you successfully fill your days with so much noise and business that you never face the inevitability of death, you never have to face the need—or even the hope—of salvation from death, right?

Till the time runs out.

The Transcendent Now

If there is a life after death, a way of existing independently of time and space, then Jesus is there right now with our Father and with all those who have died till now. Death is not an end but a transformation into a new way of being real, thinner than thought, weightier than death.

For some strange reason, I kept thinking of that new dimension of reality as precisely that: the *after*life, a life I will enter when I die, with the result that I kept thinking of it almost as if it would not begin until I got there! It's a kind of typical self-centered mistake: defining reality only in terms of its usefulness to myself. And yet, if there is a way of existing without reference to time or space, it must exist *now*. Not just for those already in it, but for us too! Even at this moment, if we are able to live in that dimension in moments of ecstasy, if we are able to contact it in prayer, if it has no reverence for the limits of time or space, then it's as much "here" as any "place" else! We are in it, even though we cannot see it, but only get hints from it, as Helen Keller was bathed in a sunshine she couldn't see but which, on the word of those who could see it, she trusted was there. And she rejoiced in it.

It is as if our way of existing (the universe and everything in it) were immersed in the midst of God's way of existing. We have our own seemingly solid space-time reality, but all of it is thoroughly saturated by that other Reality.

That's what happens when prayer really works! The more real Reality "breaks through!" That's where I am when, in moments of ecstasy, of joy, of love, my spirit swings free and fully alive in its true home. In those moments, I am in touch with the incandescent aliveness of God, an aliveness before which my human aliveness, beautiful as it is, is still a pale imitation.

Then Hopkins is right: "The world is charged with the grandeur of God!" His super reality is burning beneath the surfaces of everything I see, and the resurrected Jesus *is* behind every face I meet—no matter how unpromising it appears on the surface! Everything I do to make the spirit within me grow is intensified by its saturation with the super-aliveness of God's Spirit. Everything I do echoes infinitely; beyond my carefully hedged backyard, beyond the farthest galaxies, beyond even the idea of time and space. The true "I" within me, which rises out of the body and mind like their flowering, can't be measured by seventy years on a time line, or a speck on a cosmic map, or a small heap of temporary and eventually evanescent human accomplishments. It is when I *love* that I build up treasure no moth can eat, no time can rust!

I am a son of the Most High God!

I apologize for the profusion of apostrophes, but this is Good News indeed!

However, if you are content with a seventy-year life (at best), if you are content with the tiny confines of a neighborhood and a job, if you are content with small failures and small triumphs in a world limited to a body and a mind that will cease, then you will feel no hunger for a dimension to your life—even now—that goes beyond the remotest stars.

And it's true, you'll never know what you missed.

6. IGNORANT FEAR OF THE HUMAN COMMUNITY

The last chapter spoke of the hedges we surround ourselves with in order to keep out the distressing realizations that a larger world would force upon us: our personal negligibility in the face of time and space and death, our personal helplessness in the face of the immense world problems of hunger and war and illiteracy, our personal reluctance to challenge the materialist system that comforts our bodies and corrodes our spirits. And despite the suburban, middle-class metaphor of "hedges," this erection and maintenance of self-defenses goes on just as staunchly in the urban ghetto and in the Appalachian backwoods. It is not a calculated ignorance of a larger world which is restricted to the well-to-do. All of us, no matter what our economic or social status, stifle our longing for greener pastures because we fear to range forth and seek them lest we lose the small security we have on this side of the wall.

But, despite this fear of the unknown, of the possibly threatening Other, there is a yearning so deep and so consistent in men and women, both today and through all recorded history, that I cannot help but think it is part of human nature. That is the yearning to belong, to be a part of something bigger than the confines of one's own skin. Granted that the scope of the universe and its problems is too large and complex for us personally to want to bother about, still there is a need for some society. The men and women who are self-reliant enough (or anti-social enough) to be hermits are very few. Even though we feel it is too much to ask us to deal with or care about *all* the men and women and children on the face of the earth, the opposite extreme—having *no* one else to deal with or care about—is equally repugnant. We need others. We crave companionship. Why? Because being lonely in an uncaring universe is as fearsome a state as being naked and vulnerable before all the world's needs.

When we say that human beings need to love and to be loved, we are saying that all of us need to be vulnerable to somebody; we must take the risk of sharing with somebody; we must let down our rules for membership and our drawbridges for somebody because being totally alone is utterly insupportable. On the one hand, our urge for self-preservation is the urge to exclude—to shut out every person or problem or realization that might cause us discomfort or pain or loss. On the other hand, though, directly contradictory to that urge for self-preservation, is the equally profound urge—if not to include, at least to *be* included, to be cared for, to be not-alone. Each of us finds himself or herself, at the deepest inner level, tied by each hand to two different herds of powerful needs pulling with incredible strength in precisely opposite directions: preserving oneself from possible hurt and sharing oneself for possible love. How does one keep from being torn asunder?

To cope with these contradictory urges, each one of us, in his or her own unique way, compromises. The most fearful (and perhaps the sickest) among us invent imaginary friends, non-existent "others" with whom we can relate without the risk of being hurt by free and unpredictable others. The need to share and the fear of risk are both so strong that the only endurable alternative for such people is a non-threatening mental fabrication. Some of these people even use a false idea of God as this *alter ego*, preferring to share their time and their conversation and their life-focus with "it"—not as the challenging Father he has revealed himself to be, but as a mothering symbol, an understanding bosom and protecting arms that "won't let them hurt my baby."

Others content themselves with one friend or spouse, scrupulously tried and true, with whom they share everything. This is perhaps better than sharing with no one, but it is a pitiably cramped and nearly sterile pairing of lives, consciously excluding not only those who might threaten the union but also those who could possibly enhance it and challenge it and enrich it. Oddly, however, this you-and-me-against-the-world exclusivity is precisely what a great many adolescents and even adults are searching for with the persistence of medieval alchemists. They may not knowingly be seeking such exclusivity; they may even have a few other surface friends with whom they spend surface time and share surface communication. But the only true communication, the only true love, the only true time is what they expend on one another. This is the case with individuals who search for or, sadly, have found the one, exclusive "best friend," the soul mate. This is also the sadly cramping, dulling case with so many young people who go steady with an iron monogamy worthy of Adam and Eve. It is not unusual in such cases that when the young man, say, returns from college for a week at Christmas, his "woman" creates a poutingly jealous scene if he wants to steal one evening of their precious seven to play basketball or go out drinking beer with the boys. It is the same sickening lack of trust and fear of loss that makes a boy seethe with jealousy if "his" girl spends too long at a party talking with some interesting young man.

And, ironically, such self-protection inevitably becomes self-impoverishment. Chained by exclusivity to me, the person I love is honor-bound not to be enriched by any significant personal experiences that exclude me, and, therefore, has little or nothing fresh to share with me when we come back from our antiseptically impersonal encounters with other people. And when these two people's spirits have no other food than one another, they have thin fare indeed.

Still others are a trifle wiser. They understand, at least instinctively, that they need at least a slightly wider circle of pals, a clique, a club, a team—some group whose interests are just a bit more variegated than their own, but nonetheless dominated by a common and unthreatening interest. There is a price, of course. Not everybody in the small group will be equally appealing, but they can be tolerated for the sake of the larger comradeship, the sharing, the greater possibility of new ideas and new points of view that many unique persons can offer when they get together.

Those with even wider horizons, wider scopes of friends, responsibilities—and consequently higher risks—are, in my experience, far fewer. Those who are willing to leave behind the fragile protection of the clique and begin caring about a group as large as a class or a neighborhood or a department as an entity for which they feel personally responsible are not rare but are not frequent. To those who are more self-defensive, such people look like "do-gooders" or "self-appointed Messiahs." That derision, however, most often seems a thin veneer over the critics' envious wish that they also had the courage to live such a larger life.

Here, I think, is the sticking point. It is not unusual at all that fearful people (which is most of us) will be lured at least a few steps outside of their hedges by the need to share, at least as far as a "best friend" or a "steady" relationship and a very limited number of "buddies." But I think I can say without overgeneralization that, for most of us, going beyond that very minimal compromise is something just a bit too risky. Going even further and, say, running for the Senate is—often literally—courting suicide.

The alibis for holding back from even responsibility for a neighborhood are numberless: what good would it do; somebody else will do it; I've got my own problems; what the hell business is it of mine; I'm not smart or bold like those other guys; and on and on and on.

And all the while, outside those tiny, well-protected and exclusive little societies, a great wild and exciting life goes swirling on—a life that could be theirs for the asking.

I cease to be surprised by the unerring regularity with which, year after year, I read editorials in school papers all over the country on "Our Lack of School Spirit." Or how few risk even raising their hands in a class to question what the teacher says. "After all, it's not my job. I'm only an insignificant person." I am not surprised at the enormous amounts of money spent on anti-litter campaigns despite the still rising mountains of garbage along our streets and highways and in our parks. "I'm only one insignificant person." I am beyond surprise when I ask large groups of people how many have ever, even once, written a letter to their senator or congressman or bishop or even their pastor on any subject whatsoever. Nor am I surprised when the papers say only 50% of those elibigle voted in the last election. "I'm only an insignificant person."

When I ponder such deadening refusal to be counted, I can't help but remember the scene in *A Man for All Seasons* when the Common Man, acting as Thomas More's jailer, says he'd like to help

More but, "You got to understand, sir. I'm just a plain, simple man." And More, who is about to die because of his willingness to be counted, cries out, "Sweet Jesus! These plain, simple men!"

If my assessment of this seemingly pervasive unwillingness to risk is even remotely accurate, is it any wonder why so many people feel they live dogged, cramped, rat-race lives?

Perhaps the basis of this fear to reach out to a larger and richer society is a fear of variety. That sounds foolish because we all claim to be bored by repetition—the nine-to-five job, the numbing routine of classes, the week-after-week formula of the Mass. But if this urge for variety is so strong, I can't help but wonder why this week's *TV Guide* looks so remarkably similar to the *TV Guide* ten years ago, with the same only vaguely reworked situation comedies, detective stories and "variety" shows. If this urge for variety is so strong, I can't help but wonder why everybody sports the same only vaguely reworked hairstyles and clothes and music and food habits as everybody else, why the guy with the brushcut and the guy with the yellow socks and the guy with the violin and the guy who orders calves' liver is always "some kind of weirdo." If this urge for variety is so strong, I can't help but wonder why the majority of people I know are so hesitant to meet foreigners, work with retarded children, read books that argue against their own opinions.

We say we want variety, but by its very nature variety is threatening. It's new, unknown, perhaps a waste of time, perhaps even something that will call into question comfortably solid habits. We say we want lots and lots of friends, but a multiplicity of friends is also threatening. First of all, the more deep friendships one has, the more chances that there will be time-consuming requests for help. Besides that, the more friends one has, the more varied opinions one is going to encounter, which means one has to adapt and refocus his own dearly held opinions; it's far more exciting but also far more precarious. Something deep inside is far more comfortable not with repetition but with something *predictable*.

Part of this cowering can be blamed on the overcrowding of our cities. With so many potential muggers, rapists and con artists always lurking unpredictably out there in the faceless mob, the only shrewd stance is a very low profile. But I think this reason is a copout. In the first place, the reason that the potential marauder *can* lurk anonymously in the crowd is precisely that he *knows* the frightened sheep don't want to get involved, won't stand up to him, want just to blind themselves to anything outside their tunnel vision. In the second place, this willingness to melt into the anonymity of the faceless crowd is found just as consistently in rural areas. The need to belong and the need for protective camouflage seem to be—and always to have been—contradictory parts of the same human nature.

It is amusing to realize, however, that your best friend today was once a total stranger too.

We also say we want a rich, full life, but very

rarely do we specify what "a rich, full life" means and what will lead us to it. To many, it means in some vague way money; to others it means sex; to others it means power; to still others it means religion or literature or fame or love. It would seem, however, that the more varied and frequent experience a man or woman had of *all* areas of life, all kinds of people and customs and beliefs, the richer and fuller their lives would be. And yet most of the young people who say they want "experience" limit the scope of their experience to something as transitory as a one-shot hitch across the country, meeting a collection of people no more varied than a succession of truck drivers and hash-house waitresses whose lives have stalled far short of their dreams.

Then, almost as inevitably as dying, they return home to a job as a mechanic or clerk or housewife, with the same round of parties with the same friends who share the same interests and experiences.

But let me not seem to condemn the young people who want to hitch across the country. At least they have the guts for one brief part of their lives to reach out to strangers and in some way share their lives, or at least brush up against them. At least for a while there is some hope for them, but only if they are sensitive to the unique differences between this diner and the last, between this gas station attendant and the last. The hitchhiker's life will be enriched only if he takes time to reflect not only on what these people look like and what they talk about (which will most often be very much the same), but why they are who they are. His life—and theirs—will be enriched only if he can persuade them to open their inner selves to him and he is willing to open his inner self to them. Not everyone has the finesse and the personality and the knowledge of words to do that. Not everyone has the courage.

Moreover, one needn't travel cross-country to find a group of people infinitely varied to the sensitive eye and spirit. They are right there at your elbows all the time, brushing anonymously past the gates of your self-protection—in the same classroom, in the same office, in the same neighborhood. Even, surprisingly, in the same family. Even in the same church. And all of it is only one perilous footstep away.

The Threatening Church

If I had to isolate the one most immediate reason why so many young adults are drifting away from the Church today, I think it would focus close to what this chapter has attempted to deal with: a fear of risking oneself beyond one's safe circle of friends, a craving for the richer life and an unwillingness to seek out a richer life.

The only contact most Catholics have with the Church in any given week is Sunday Mass. When the Sunday Catholic sits there in the normally large congregation of people, people usually as uptight and self-protective as he, something rings false in the

Gospel readings and homilies that imply that the core of Christianity is love. And surely calling this assemblage a "celebration" seems a misnomer. Irritating as the collection basket is, it is at least impersonal and non-intimidating—unlike the requests to sing out loud and strong, or of the handshake of peace with faceless strangers who could drop dead tomorrow and we'd neither hear about it nor care. Isn't it true that when some hotshot priest tries to draw the congregation into some more meaningful, more personal, more self-forgetful activities, we all —young as well as old—get just a bit resentful? And if the young people who tell me they're so all-fired eager for Mass to be as alive as a rock concert really mean what they say, why do I always see them standing at the back of the Church by the door?

If the Mass at one's own parish is deadly dull— and not a few of them truly are—what prevents anyone from shopping around in other parishes for a more meaningful liturgy? Inertia, for one thing. And our old pal Calculated Ignorance. If I were to go to a Mass that really swings, I may have to get *involved* in the bloody Church! It'll mean evenings away from *Kojack* so I can help immigrants learn English or something like that. It'll mean the embarrassment of knocking on doors and asking for donations for something like Catholic Charities. It'll mean reading that damn Bible that I said in school I'd never open again, and putting my head on the block for things like anti-abortion bills and complicating my life even more than it is now. Too much.

"You got to understand, sir. I'm just a plain, simple man." It's better, in the end, to settle for the small life, the uncomplicated life, even the dull life rather than risk the pittance of a life I have in order to have Everything.

It would be quite normal for someone to say; "How dare you say I have a 'pittance of a life'." Perhaps you don't. But if there is the slightest suspicion that you could open it more, enrich it more, risk it more, perhaps Jesus is talking to you when he says, "Come and see."

"I have come that they may have life, and have it more abundantly." If Christianity does not pervade your life, enliven it more abundantly than the lives of the people you see around you, perhaps you have never experienced what Christianity truly means, what Christianity can truly do to your life. If you say that such a thing is not possible, then perhaps your calculated ignorance may be blinder than you'd thought.

One can call to a friend at the side of a lake, "C'mon in! The water's beautiful!" But only the prospective swimmer can let go of the solid security of the dock. One can stand outside the cramped but comfortable, dark but womb-like cave and cry, "Come out! The sun dance is a miracle! You won't believe it!" But only the denizen of the cave can forswear its assurances and buckle his courage to sacrifice the safely dull darkness for the infinitely varied Light.

7. CODA: SURFACES

I sometimes wonder if the greatest obstacle to people's acceptance of the Church as an enriching avenue to God and to their fellow human beings may not be the Church herself, as we see her concretized in our every-week lives.

There are some who look upon the Church as if she hadn't changed one iota since they lost interest in her: the same endless stories of Nazi nuns and money-grubbing sermons and aloofness from the real problems of the world—this despite the liberation of nuns, the conscious attempts to relate homilies to the Gospel, the priests and nuns who have been imprisoned for involvement in "the real problems of the world." Others, in an attempt to make the Church more "relevant," to lure back the vacationing Catholics and hold the young within the Church just a bit longer, seem to have compromised all the grit and spine out of being a Catholic: larding over liturgies with purple-patch rock groups, watering down any stiffness of stance into mere ethical humanism, tolerating any position—no matter how bizarre—so that, in standing for everything, we end by standing for nothing. Still others cling to every jot and tittle of the Law with the tenacity of mountain climbers: refusing to adapt to the receptivities of the audiences at Mass, treating every moral question from reading *Penthouse* to having an abortion with the same fiery fulminations, siding fearfully with the forces not of restraint but of immobility.

The surface confusion becomes too much; the man or woman of awakening faith finds no root in the rocky ground of conservativism or the shifting sands of liberalism. And the beginnings of faith wither and die.

The cause, I think, is in mistaking the surface for the essence, the skin of the body for the Spirit that animates it. Both the leaders of the Church and the members of the Church who are wondering whether to stay on or not seem to make the same mistake.

Pastors and bishops and involved lay people, whether conservative or liberal, battle over the sur-faces—how much improvisation in the Mass, what kinds of political activity are "seemly," whether to post signs saying no one is admitted wearing ber-muda shorts. These hardly seem to be the problems that the original Christians troubled themselves with. "They looked up and saw only Jesus."

The shaky adherents—and some of the im-movably firm church-goers—are troubled by equally surface difficulties: the size of buildings and the smothering numbers at Sunday Mass, the curate's stereo set, the nun in grammar school who misunder-stood. But more importantly, their only connection with the Church is almost always the single hour they think they are allowing God into their otherwise occupied lives—Sunday Mass. Everything—the entire burden of their continued attachment to the Church—depends on how well that one hour a week "pays off." A large number, especially of younger people, endure it for awhile, miss a few times with far less soul-wracking guilt than they'd expected, and finally, one Sunday, it's just not worth getting out of bed for any more.

Is that a mortal sin? I wonder. How can one be guilty of breaking up a relationship that may never in any true sense have existed? How can one be called to task for deserting a spouse one has never even really met, much less really accepted as a person one loves? How many of those, old or young, who drift away from Catholic practice, ever really penetrated below the surfaces of candles and homilies and ritual to a *personal* relationship with the God we come to celebrate each Sunday? (And Monday and Tuesday.) Of course, if the Mass is merely routine, if one has no real love for or even knowledge of the Guest of Honor, it is ludicrous in his eyes even to call it a "celebration."

In the course of these pages, I have asserted that the deepest cause of unbelief is a calculated ignorance, refusing for fear of the consequences to one's own security to consider the facts that one has been gifted with existence by a God who deserves our gratitude for that gift, that one is capable of sin and is therefore in need of Someone to whom he can apologize and be forgiven, that enslavement to the false gods of materialism dehumanizes him, that refusal to face the fact of death makes him unaware of

his life as a spirit enlivened by being infused with the
aliveness of his transcendent Father, that fear of the
human family shrinks the scope of his life-giving
power to love.

But the soil in which all these weed-roots thrive
is the soil of inertia. It is just too much effort to peel
away the surfaces of things and probe their inner
meanings. It takes too long to learn how to pray
with any profit. It is easier to learn how to do book-
keeping or baking or skiing. It is easier to stay on
the surfaces, and you will never be taken in. But not
being taken in means you are left out.

The more I ponder how to overcome that slug-
gishness, the more I become convinced that all the
means at the disposal of the Catholic educator—discussions and film strips, homilies and retreats, even
the Mass and the Scriptures themselves—are merely
means, not ends. And the means we push hardest—
Mass and the Scriptures—are really very much "ac-
quired tastes." It is only the convinced believer who
can cut through whatever surface difficulties they
may have into the Spirit who animates them.

For a long time I chafed at religious teachers
who turned their classes into forests of banners with
quotes from e. e. cummings and who seemed merely
to be filling out the time with films that were inducements to widen one's horizons only on the horizontal
human level, with no transcendent, divine dimension
whatsoever. And then I realized how wrong I was. If
the message of Jesus was, "I come that you may
have life, and have it more abundantly," then one

must have some spark of human life before the fire Jesus came to cast from heaven can take hold. It is difficult for the beginner to see Jesus behind the surfaces of his brother or sister being, when he has not yet acknowledged that this person *is* his brother or sister being. It is even more difficult when he has yet even to acknowledge that this person is *there*.

Therefore, I would beg the indulgence of those who are angry that kids coming out of Catholic schools now aren't sufficiently eager for Catholic practice. If a good many of them are beginning to suspect a wider world than their own hedged backyards the Christian schools have not failed completely, and these young people may be ripe for a far richer Catholicism than their elders ever knew.

But what do we do with them then? If the only inducements to take their new-found humanity further into a humanity enlivened by the Spirit of God are soul-less Sunday rituals, they will either remain on that humanistic level or will turn to some other source—Zen, drugs, social action, communes—that seems to offer greater promise of spiritual growth.

Very simply, then, let me conclude: Until we teach our young people to pray—not merely rote prayers or even ritualized prayers, but a prayer that will bring them into contact with the wellspring Spirit of Light who swells within them—the roots of unbelief will thrive and grow strong in the resultant darkness.